To: _____

From: _____

Date: _____

The Gift
The Gospel for Children

Published in Dallas, Texas, by Pathway to Victory, the media ministry of First Baptist Church Dallas. 1707 San Jacinto, Dallas, TX 75201. www.ptv.org.

ISBN 978-0-692-80250-2

Directed by Nate Curtis
Designed by Patrick Heatherington
Edited by Robin Crouch
Illustrated by Lisa S. Reed

Printed and bound in the United States of America.

THE GIFT

THE GOSPEL FOR CHILDREN

DR. ROBERT JEFFRESS

A Message To Adults

From Dr. Robert Jeffress

The most important thing we can do for our children and grandchildren, nieces and nephews, is share God's gift of salvation with them. In this book I present the Gospel—the Good News— that Jesus died for their sins and rose from the dead. Our prayer is that every child and adult understand and accept this free gift.

In this book we talk about the gift in two parts. Part 1 is titled "Receiving God's Gift." In it, I present the Gospel in a way that is easy to understand. You should read it to a child in one sitting. At the end of this section, your child will have a chance to receive God's forgiveness and the gift of eternal life.

Part 2 of this book is titled "Enjoying God's Gift." In it, I explain how we should live after we have become a Christian. This part of the book is divided into chapters. You should read one chapter a night to your child. At the end of each chapter, he or she will have a chance to answer questions about what he or she has just heard.

I hope that you and the children in your life enjoy this book. I enjoyed writing it. We look forward to hearing how God has used it to introduce the children in your life (and maybe even you) to God's free gift of salvation in Jesus Christ.

Sincerely,

Dr. Robert Jeffress
Senior Pastor, First Baptist Church, Dallas, Texas
Bible Teacher, *Pathway to Victory*

PART 1

Receiving God's Gift

GOD HAS A GIFT FOR YOU.

You already know that God gives you every new day. You already know that He presents you with each new opportunity.

Now God wants you to know something else. He has something special for you . . .

. . . a gift that lasts forever.

For by grace you have been
saved through faith;
and that not of yourselves,
it is the gift of God.

— **Ephesians 2:8**

GOD HAS ALWAYS KNOWN YOU.

All life on this earth comes from God the Father. He knew you before you were born.

And all life on this earth comes to an end. The Bible says that each of us will die. After death, some people go to heaven, where Jesus is. People in heaven enjoy all the great things God has planned.

But some people don't go to heaven when they die. They go to hell, where the devil lives, and they suffer. They can never find a way to heaven from this terrible place.

This is the most important news you will ever hear: the Bible says you can make sure you go to heaven.

Before I formed you in the womb I knew you,
And before you were born I consecrated you.
— **Jeremiah 1:5**

WHAT DO I NEED TO DO?

You can't get to heaven by doing good things. Not even if you feed every poor person. Not even if you give away everything you have. Not even if you spend your whole life helping others.

The Bible says, in order to get to heaven when you die, there are **four things** you have to understand in your mind and believe in your heart.

As you read the next few pages, imagine your whole mind opening. Imagine your whole heart opening as well.

> Serve Him with a whole heart and a willing mind; for the Lord searches all hearts, and understands every intent of the thoughts.
> — **1 Chronicles 28:9**

1. EVERYBODY SINS.

This is the first thing you must understand and believe: **Everybody sins.** Everyone is guilty of sin. Sin means disobeying God's rules.

Your parents make rules for your good. If you obey your parents' rules, things usually go well. If you break them, your parents punish you.

It's the same way with God. He gave us rules for how we should live. These are good rules. The problem is, we have all broken God's rules.

For all have sinned and fall short of the glory of God.

— Romans 3:23

2. WE DESERVE TO BE PUNISHED FOR OUR SINS.

This is the second thing you must understand: **We deserve to be punished for our sins.**

What happens when you break your parents' rules? They punish you. Maybe they spank you. Maybe they send you to your room, or put you in time-out, or take your cell phone from you.

It's the same way with God. We have all broken God's rules. We deserve to be punished. But the punishment for breaking God's rules is far worse than a spanking. It means being sent to hell when we die. Hell is a terrible place completely separated from God. And it lasts forever. Forever is a long, long time.

It's a permanent time-out.

For the wages of sin is death.

— Romans 6:23

3. JESUS TOOK THE PUNISHMENT FOR OUR SINS.

The Bible tells us that God loved the world very much—and that includes you. So much that He sent us His Son.

Can you imagine giving away your only child?

The prophets had told of this child. An angel appeared to both Mary and Joseph about the coming of this baby.

And the heavenly host sang when Jesus was born.

And she gave birth to her firstborn son; and she wrapped Him in cloths, and laid Him in a manger, because there was no room for them in the inn.

— Luke 2:7

God sent His Son to earth for one reason: to take the punishment for your sin so you could go to heaven when you die.

This is the third thing you must understand and believe: **Jesus took the punishment for our sins.**

For God so loved the world, that He gave His only begotten Son, that whoever believes in Him shall not perish, but have eternal life.

— **John 3:16**

Imagine you have a brother or sister who broke a rule. Imagine they are in serious trouble. You want to help, and the only way is to take your brother or sister's place.

Would you take a spanking for another person's lie? That's exactly what Jesus did. Jesus Christ took the punishment from God that you and I deserve for our sins. He gave His life in your place.

Throughout His life, Jesus obeyed His father's commands.

He never sinned.

Jesus never did anything wrong, but He was willing to die on the cross and take the punishment from God that you and I deserve for our sins.

This is God's gift to you.

> But God demonstrates His own love toward us, in that while we were yet sinners, Christ died for us.
> — **Romans 5:8**

4. WE MUST RECEIVE GOD'S GIFT OF FORGIVENESS.

So far, we have talked about three things you must understand and believe.

1. Everybody sins.
2. We deserve to be punished for our sins.
3. Jesus took the punishment for our sins.

People can believe all these things and still go to hell when they die. So the fourth and last thing is this: **We must receive God's gift of forgiveness.**

Imagine someone comes to your house with a present. "This is for you," he says. "I chose it for you." That person has the gift in his hands. He holds it out, toward you. What must happen for this gift to be yours? You have to reach out and accept the gift for it to become yours.

In the same way, you have to reach out and accept God's gift of forgiveness for it to become yours.

But the free gift of God is eternal life in Christ Jesus our Lord.

— **Romans 6:23**

NOW IS THE TIME TO PRAY.

You can open your heart and receive God's gift of forgiveness. How? By telling God you would like to receive His gift of salvation. Here is a prayer you can say to God to do that.

Dear God,

Thank you for loving me. I know that I have sinned. And I'm truly sorry for the bad things I've done. But I believe that you sent Jesus to die on the cross for my sins.

Right now, I'm trusting in Jesus and what He did for me to save me from my sins. Thank you for forgiving me. Please help me live the rest of my life obeying you. In Jesus' name I pray. Amen.

But as many as received Him, to them He gave the right to become children of God, even to those who believe in His name.

— John 1:12

CONGRATULATIONS!

You have just received the best gift of your life!

But this is just the beginning.

Now is the time to learn to enjoy God's gift to you.

PART 2

Enjoying God's Gift

Chapter 1
YOU'RE SAVED!

Now you'll begin a new "walk" in life. Sometimes this is called a "walk of faith." You will feel strong emotions. You will often have more questions than answers. And you'll want help along the way.

Take time to learn from the Bible. Seek help from other Christians. And don't expect changes to happen in your life overnight. Like any journey, you will grow stronger with each step. As you grow, record your joys and challenges.

Try your hand at keeping a journal of faith. You can start by making notes in this portion of the book. A new strength awaits!

> Yet those who wait for the Lord
> Will gain new strength;
> They will mount up with wings like eagles,
> They will run and not get tired,
> They will walk and not become weary.

> — Isaiah 40:31

THE GIFT THE GOSPEL FOR CHILDREN

Today's date: _____

The most exciting thing about this day is . . .

_____

_____

_____

_____

_____

Name the first person you told about getting saved.

_____

What was his or her reaction to your good news?

_____

_____

Write down the book, chapter number, and verse
number of the first Bible passage you looked up after
being saved. _____

_____

_____

_____

_____

Chapter 2

TAKE EVERYTHING TO GOD IN PRAYER.

Now you belong to Jesus, and His love gives you room to pray about anything. Take your problems to Him. Tell Him your hopes and dreams. Remember to pray for others. And remember to thank Him for your blessings. There are hundreds of helpful Bible verses about prayer. They will help you understand how to pray. God is always ready to listen to you.

Jesus' followers, the disciples, asked Him to teach them to pray. He taught them the Lord's Prayer. Try to memorize the Lord's Prayer if you haven't already. Just talk to God.

Our Father who is in heaven, hallowed
be Your name.
Your kingdom come. Your will be done,
On earth as it is in heaven.
Give us this day our daily bread. And
forgive us our debts,
as we also have forgiven our debtors.
And do not lead us into temptation, but
deliver us from evil.
For Yours is the kingdom and the power
and the glory forever. Amen.

— **Matthew 6:9–13**

MY PRAYER JOURNAL.

Today's date: _____

List the things you are thankful for.

_____
_____
_____
_____
_____
_____
_____

List the things that worry you.

_____
_____
_____
_____
_____
_____
_____
_____
_____

What are your hopes?

_____

_____

_____

_____

_____

_____

_____

_____

List how God answered your prayers.

_____

_____

_____

_____

_____

_____

_____

_____

Chapter 3
SHARE THE GOOD NEWS.

Becoming a Christian is exciting. Your life feels brand-new. Your heart fills with thanks to God. And you want to share this gift with others. The Bible says not to be ashamed of talking about Jesus. So take some time to get ready to share your faith. Remind yourself of the four things you had to believe and understand:

1. *Everybody sins.*
2. *We deserve to be punished for our sins.*
3. *Jesus took the punishment for our sins.*
4. *We must receive God's gift of forgiveness.*

God wants you to help others understand that they can be saved, too. Sharing the Good News of salvation is also called "sharing the gospel."

And He said to them, "Go into all the world and preach the gospel to all creation."

           — Mark 16:15

Practice writing the four things to believe and understand.

_____

_____

_____

_____

What does "accepting the gift of forgiveness" mean?

_____

_____

_____

Think about how you felt before you were saved. Now write about the differences in your life since you accepted God's gift.

_____

_____

_____

Name a person you'd like to tell about this gift.

_____

Chapter 4

MAKE GOING TO CHURCH A HABIT.

The Bible tells Christians to spend time together. This is called "fellowship." Fellowship builds us up. It encourages love and good works. In fellowship, we give comfort and grow stronger together.

God's place for Christians to fellowship is called the church. A church is not just a building. It is a group of Christians who gather together to worship God, learn more about the Bible, encourage each other, and work together to share the message of salvation with others.

Every Christian needs to be part of a church. If you don't have a church home, find one. Ask whoever gave you this book about his or her church. Most churches have groups of children just like you.

Jesus promises to be there when we gather together.

THE GIFT THE GOSPEL FOR CHILDREN

"For where two or three have gathered together in My name, I am there in their midst."

— **Matthew 18:20**

Write the names of your church friends.

_____

_____

Talk about how you and a friend grow together as Christians.

_____

_____

_____

What do you pray about together?

_____

_____

_____

Name some friends that you would like to invite to your church.

_____

_____

Chapter 5

FAITH COMES WITH A USER MANUAL.

The Bible is sometimes called Scripture or the scriptures. But we usually call the Bible "God's Word" because it is God's message to us.

And because the Bible comes from God, everything in it is true. You can believe everything the Bible says!

Take time to read your Bible every day. Pray before you read. Ask God to help you understand. Don't give up when you don't understand something. Ask your minister or Sunday school teacher if you need a little more help. And keep reading.

Just like a user manual for faith, the Bible answers your questions. And as your understanding grows, you will become stronger and wiser.

All Scripture is inspired by God and profitable for teaching, for reproof, for correction, for training.

— 2 Timothy 3:16

Name the book, chapter number, and verse number(s) for your favorite Bible verse.

_____

Write the whole verse or verses.

_____

_____

_____

_____

Explain at least one way this verse affects your life.

_____

_____

_____

_____

Keep a list here of Bible verses that you don't yet understand. Mark them off once you know what they mean.

_____

_____

_____

_____

Chapter 6
LOVE AS HE LOVES.

Jesus gave us clear teachings about our behavior. He felt so strongly about one teaching that He called it a "new commandment." He said we are to love one another *the same way* He loves us.

Remember this the next time you have a problem with someone. You might think about yelling. You may feel like slamming a door. You might even want to take all your toys and go home.

Instead, think about Christ's love. Look at others through His eyes. Treat the people in your life with this kind of love. Jesus said this love shows others that we are His followers.

A new commandment I give to you, that you love one another, even as I have loved you, that you also love one another.

— John 13:34

Talk about a time when you had a problem with a family member or friend.

_____

_____

_____

What did you do?

_____

_____

_____

What did he or she do?

_____

_____

_____

How did you feel afterward?

_____

_____

_____

Chapter 7
BE KIND ALWAYS.

Jesus talked about the day when we will meet Him face-to-face. In heaven, He will remind us about how we helped "the least" of His people. "The least" means those who suffer.

He will talk about the time we gave Him food when He was hungry. He will mention when He was thirsty, and we gave Him something to drink. He will tell of other times He suffered, and then say exactly what we did to help.

Then Jesus will remind us that when we did these things, we *did this* to Him. So be ready to have this conversation with Jesus in heaven. You know you'll be there, because you accepted God's gift of forgiveness.

"Truly I say to you, to the extent that you did it to one of these brothers of Mine, even the least of them, you did it to Me."

— Matthew 25:40

Think about people in your neighborhood, church, or town who suffer. Write down at least three of their names.

_____

_____

_____

How do they suffer?

_____

_____

_____

What have you done—or what can you do—to help these people?

_____

_____

_____

Chapter 8
LEARN TO SERVE OTHERS.

The Bible says that Jesus "took the form of a servant" on this earth. This means He served others. And He told His followers that they, too, must be servants.

Imagine yourself in Jesus's shoes as you walk through your life. Does your mom need someone to take out the trash? Do it without being asked. Can you see an elderly person trying to work in the yard? Try to help that person. Is there someone in the lunchroom sitting all alone? Pull up a chair and start a conversation.

Being a servant means being unselfish. It means having a willing heart to help others. It means trusting God's will in our lives.

For we are His workmanship, created in Christ Jesus for good works, which God prepared beforehand so that we would walk in them.

— Ephesians 2:10

What happened the last time you were unselfish?

_____

_____

_____

What did the person say and do afterward?

_____

_____

_____

Circle the feelings that you had while being a servant.

Peace   Joy   Love

List three ways you can be a better servant with loved ones.

_____

_____

_____

Chapter 9

WHEN YOU ARE HAPPY, PRAISE THE LORD.

We're quick to tell God when we're worried. We almost immediately pray when we want something. But when we're happy, what should we do? How do we fit God into our joy? We praise Him!

You can sing His praise, pray it, or speak it out loud. Praise shows God that you understand how great He is. It also shows that we are mindful of Him at all times—not just when we need His help.

So the next time you realize you're feeling just fine, take a moment to praise the Lord.

Is anyone cheerful? Let him sing praise.

— **James 5:13**

Write about the last time you felt joyful.

_____

_____

_____

Where were you and who was with you?

_____

_____

_____

What caused your happiness?

_____

_____

_____

Now list three things that make you cheerful.

_____

_____

_____

_____

Chapter 10
FORGIVE OTHERS.

All of us are going to be hurt by somebody. Don't try to get even.

This can be hard. You might feel angry at the other person for hurting you. Ask God to help you forgive them. Remember, God has forgiven us, so we must also forgive them. Pray for the other person and let God punish whoever hurt you.

The Bible even says we should bless mean people. That means do something nice for them. The nicest thing we can do for them is to pray for them. God promises that He will bless us when we do this.

Be kind to one another, tender-hearted, forgiving each other, just as God in Christ also has forgiven you.

— Ephesians 4:32

Name a bully you know.

_____

Write down one mean thing he or she says to others.

_____

_____

List some bad things that this person does to others.

_____

_____

_____

Write his or her name in this prayer, and read it silently to God.

Heavenly Father, thank you for your promises. I want to bless _____ today. And I ask you to help me be patient with all bullies. Show me how to be kind when others are mean. Amen.

Chapter 11

SAY NO TO SIN.
MAKE YOUR ESCAPE.

Satan is God's enemy. God's Word says that Satan will do everything he can to get you to sin. When you want to do something wrong, that is Satan tempting you to sin.

But God wants you to learn to say "no" to Satan's temptation and "yes" to what is right.

The Bible calls this a "trial" or a "test." If we pass the test, God promises to reward us. And God even promises to help us pass the test!

Here are several ways you can turn from sin and do what is right:

1. Pray: ask God to help you.
2. Look for a way out that God will provide.
3. Hang around friends who want to please God.
4. Memorize Bible verses: this will train your brain and heart to do what is right.

No temptation has overtaken you but such as is common to man; and God is faithful, who will not allow you to be tempted beyond what you are able, but with the temptation will provide the way of escape also, so that you will be able to endure it.

— 1 Corinthians 10:13

Name a time when you sinned after you were saved.

_____

What happened?

_____

_____

_____

_____

How did you feel about it afterward?

_____

_____

_____

_____

If you haven't asked for forgiveness yet, do that now.
Write about what you'll do if this trial happens again.

_____

_____

_____

_____

_____

_____

THE GIFT   THE GOSPEL FOR CHILDREN

Name a time when you walked away from a sin
without committing it.

_____

_____

_____

_____

What happened?

_____

_____

_____

Where were you?

_____

_____

_____

_____

What was your escape route?

_____

_____

_____

_____

Chapter 12
IT'S A CRAZY WORLD.

The Bible tells us there will be problems on this earth. Jesus says to be happy anyway. He has already won our battles for us.

When you hear about scary events, when you read about bad news in the world, have faith in Christ. God holds the world in His hands. He created it, He loves it, and His will is done on earth.

If you find yourself worrying about the world, remember that's not your job. Pray about it. And be helpful if there is something you can do in your own neighborhood to help. You can walk in peace because you have received God's gift of everlasting life.

"These things I have spoken to you, so that in Me you may have peace. In the world you have tribulation, but take courage; I have overcome the world."

— John 16:33

Write about something in the world that scares or worries you.

_____

_____

_____

_____

_____

Now remember Jesus's promise. Close your eyes and thank Him for already solving this problem. Feel the peace He promises you. Write a thank you prayer.

_____

_____

_____

_____

_____

_____

MY PRAYER JOURNAL.

Today's date: _____

List the things you are thankful for.

_____
_____
_____
_____
_____
_____
_____

List the things that worry you.

_____
_____
_____
_____
_____
_____
_____
_____

What are your hopes?

_____

_____

_____

_____

_____

_____

_____

_____

_____

List how God answered your prayers.

_____

_____

_____

_____

_____

_____

_____

_____

_____

_____

MY PRAYER JOURNAL.

Today's date: _____

List the things you are thankful for.

_____
_____
_____
_____
_____
_____
_____

List the things that worry you.

_____
_____
_____
_____
_____
_____
_____
_____
_____

What are your hopes?

_____

_____

_____

_____

_____

_____

_____

_____

List how God answered your prayers.

_____

_____

_____

_____

_____

_____

_____

_____

MY PRAYER JOURNAL.

Today's date: _____

List the things you are thankful for.

_____
_____
_____
_____
_____
_____
_____
_____

List the things that worry you.

_____
_____
_____
_____
_____
_____
_____
_____
_____
_____

What are your hopes?

_____

_____

_____

_____

_____

_____

_____

_____

List how God answered your prayers.

_____

_____

_____

_____

_____

_____

_____

_____

DR. ROBERT JEFFRESS is Senior Pastor of the 13,000-member First Baptist Church, Dallas, Texas and a Fox News Contributor. He is also an adjunct professor at Dallas Theological Seminary.

Dr. Jeffress has made more than 2,000 guest appearances on various radio and television programs and regularly appears on major mainstream media outlets, such as Fox News Channel's "Fox and Friends," "The O'Reilly Factor," "Hannity," "Lou Dobbs Tonight," and "Judge Jeanine," also ABC's "Good Morning America," and HBO's "Real Time with Bill Maher."

Dr. Jeffress hosts a daily radio program, *Pathway to Victory*, that is heard nationwide on over 800 stations in major markets such as Dallas-Fort Worth, New York City, Chicago, Los Angeles, Washington, D.C., Houston, Portland, Denver and Seattle. His weekly television program can be seen in 195 countries and on 11,283 cable and satellite systems throughout the world, including China and on the Trinity Broadcasting Network and Daystar.

Dr. Jeffress is the author of 23 books including *When Forgiveness Doesn't Make Sense, Perfect Ending, Countdown to the Apocalypse*, and his newest book, *Not All Roads Lead to Heaven*.

THE GIFT — THE GOSPEL FOR CHILDREN

Dr. Jeffress recently led the congregation in the completion of a $135 million re-creation of its downtown campus. The project is the largest in modern church history and serves as a "spiritual oasis" covering six blocks of downtown Dallas. Dr. Jeffress graduated from Southwestern Baptist Theological Seminary with a D.Min., a Th.M. from Dallas Theological Seminary, and a B.S. degree from Baylor University.

In May 2010, he was awarded a Doctor of Divinity degree from Dallas Baptist University. In June 2011, Dr. Jeffress received the Distinguished Alumnus of the Year award from Southwestern Baptist Theological Seminary.

Dr. Jeffress and his wife Amy have two daughters, Julia and Dorothy, and a son-in-law, Ryan Sadler.

DR. ROBERT JEFFRESS, SENIOR PASTOR AND BIBLE TEACHER, FIRST BAPTIST CHURCH DALLAS